Business by the Book
Leadership and Management Principles from the Life of Christ

Workbook

Business By The Book Workbook
Published by Guy Thing Press
P.O. Box 827
Roanoke, TX 76262

This book or parts thereof may not be reproduced in any form, stored in a retrieval system, or transmitted in any form by any means - electronic, mechanical, photocopy, recording, or otherwise - without prior written permission of the publisher, except as provided by United States of America copyright law.

Guy Thing Press books my be purchased in bulk for educational, business, fund-raising, or sales promotional use. For more information, please contact Guy Thing Press.

Please visit us at www.guythingpress.com

Copyright © 2008 by Guy Thing Press
All Rights Reserved

Printed in the United States of America

ISBN-13:   978-0-9818337-4-3
ISBN-10:   0-9818337-4-3

Scripture taken from the New King James Version. Copyright © 1982 by Thomas Nelson, Inc. Used by permission. All rights reserved.

Contents

Section 1: Principles for Life 1

Section 2: Principles of Leadership 9

Section 3: Principles of Longevity 20

Section 1
Principles for Life

Business by the Book

1. What are the three aspects to a plan?
   _____
   _____
   _____

2. Most people spend their lives seeking the great _____ but never stop to ask _____.

3. You have to have more than just a good _____ if you want to leave a _____ behind for those that follow on after you.

4. What three components did Christ have?
   _____
   _____

5. When Jesus walked the earth, he spent 30 years having His _____ _____, _____. He didn't have to pray for what was coming, he had to _____ for it.

6. What is the difference between an ordinary person and an extraordinary person?
   _____

7. What proof is found in your preparation?
   _____
   _____

Section 1
Principles for Life

8. Why is the leadership style of Christ considered out of place in today's society?
_____
_____
_____

9. Jesus was a man under _____. He went about doing the will of _____
_____.

10. According to Christ, how was a disciple known?
_____
_____

11. Jesus was a man under authority with a greater love for _____ and what His Father wanted than the need to have _____
_____.

12. When it came down to crunch time with Christ, you were either _____ or _____, and _____ were responsible for that choice.

13. Why is a vision so important?
_____
_____
_____
_____

14. What steps are involved in making a vision plan?
_____
_____

15. What will happen if you lose sight of the goal?
_____

16. The catch cry of _____ is not a reflection of your schedule, but of your _____.

17. What is not part of the sacrifice for your job, vision, or passion?
_____

18. All your _____ and all your _____ and all your _____ and all your _____ have very real world implications.

19. Jesus spent time with people _____ constantly. Through His life, He deliberately made an effort to _____.

20. What important principle did Jesus teach His team about serving?
_____
_____
_____
_____

21. Jesus said that the _____ will never become greater than the _____.

22. You will never rise above the _____ of your mentors.

Section 1
Principles for Life

23. What important questions can you ask yourself when choosing whom to submit to mentally?
_____
_____
_____
_____
_____
_____

24. What does it mean to be a student of history?
_____
_____

25. How can being a student of history benefit you?
_____
_____

26. Search out history for the _____ that can _____, _____, and _____ you in the way you should go?

Business by the Book

Section 1
Principles for Life

Key Point Review

1. What does a plan achieve for you?

2. Why do you need to have more than just a good idea to leave behind a legacy?

3. Why did Christ have to spend so long having his character honed?

4. How was Jesus a man under authority?

5. What five things should you do to make a vision plan?

6. In what ways can you seek to disengage from the world and reengage with yourself and your family?
___
___
___
___

7. As you move up the corporate ladder, why should you force yourself to stay in touch with those who serve you?
___
___
___

8. What happens when we accept other men's rationalizations for their failures?
___
___

Section 2
Principles of Leadership

Business by the Book

1. No People = _____.

2. New Project = _____.

3. What mistake do businesses make when starting new projects?
   _____
   _____
   _____
   _____

4. What did King Solomon say regarding poverty?
   _____
   _____
   _____
   _____

5. If someone cannot steward _____, what makes you think they can steward _____?

6. Your leaders need to come _____.

7. What is one of the key indicators of your leaders' personal discipleship?
   _____
   _____

Section 2
Principles of Leadership

8. During what times should you cut your losses and move on?
_____
_____
_____

9. Not everybody is going to _____ you. Not everybody is going to _____ from you. Not every idea that you have is going to be _____.

10. Why should you cut your losses rather than keep trying to make something work?
_____
_____
_____

11. You will always pay for your _____. You just shouldn't have to go _____ doing it.

12. According to Jesus, what must you do in order to become great?
_____
_____

13. How will you, the key leader, change the culture of your organization and how will you notice it?
_____
_____
_____

14. You are only a success after you have _____ yourself with or _____ a successor.

15. How did Christ teach the disciples?
_____
_____
_____
_____

16. Life lessons are always best learned _____ instead of in a _____ or before a review board.

17. What does it show when you actively train and teach others?
_____
_____

18. What does it say when you train others?
_____
_____

19. What is the biggest thing you can do to ensure sound ongoing staff and personal relationships?
_____
_____

Section 2
Principles of Leadership

20. What is _____ gains value, but what _____ loses value. It is as true of cars and real estate as it is of _____.

21. What do you need when starting a new adventure?
   _____
   _____

22. When Jesus chose Judas, what was Jesus responsible for and what was Judas responsible for?
   _____
   _____
   _____
   _____

23. How did Jesus challenge His disciples in the training process?
   _____
   _____
   _____

24. How did Christ handle the errors that His disciples made?
   _____
   _____
   _____
   _____

25. What is the worst thing you can do with any new growth or expansion program?
   _____
   _____

26. To what are people usually committed?
_____
_____
_____

27. Sometimes it is best not to rebuke someone for being negative, but just simply _____
_____.

28. What does the term Generational Wealth mean?
_____
_____
_____

29. God never gives authority without _____, and neither should we. The greater the _____, the greater the _____ must be.

30. What are the different ways in which Christ referred to the Kingdom of God?
_____
_____
_____
_____

31. What is effective communication?
_____
_____

Section 2
Principles of Leadership

32. You don't _____ to leadership at the _____ of others, but as a result of _____ others.

33. What is meant by the term "team effort"?
_____
_____

Business by the Book

Section 2
Principles of Leadership

Key Point Review

1. To start a new project, you need new _____.

2. Christ never told us not to attempt the impossible, but instead told us to be aware that it would _____.

3. What qualifier did God put in place to see if we are ready/able/capable of being a steward over next level things?
   _____
   _____

4. Why is it important to review fiscal performance of a potential candidate or employee?
   _____
   _____
   _____

5. Why is it important to be able to cut your losses?
   _____
   _____
   _____

6. Explain the importance of serving and what it has to do with you as a key leader?
   _____
   _____
   _____

7. Why should you take the time to teach and train your team?
   _____
   _____
   _____

8. What is the importance of gratitude in your relationships?
   _____
   _____
   _____
   _____

9. What are some things to keep in mind when selecting your key staff?
   _____
   _____
   _____
   _____

10. Why is it important to praise in public and rebuke in private?
    _____
    _____
    _____
    _____

11. How does communication encourage commitment?
    _____
    _____

Section 2
Principles of Leadership

12. Why should you give honor?
_____
_____

Section 2
Principles of Leadership

Section 3
Principles of Longevity

1. Where is the true gauge of a person's character given?
   _____
   _____

2. When you _____ in someone, or trust someone, you are doing more than just believing in who they are. The essence of that trust is traced back to the fact that you _____ _____ - you just trust their _____.

3. When faced with opportunities, advice, or even the desire to lie, what should your second reaction be and why?
   _____
   _____
   _____

4. What does it mean to have integrity?
   _____

5. What is the only way to have integrity toward the teachings of Christ?
   _____
   _____

6. Self _____ is always the end product of self _____.

7. What does it mean to compromise?
   _____
   _____

Section 3
Principles of Longevity

8. Take some stress, add some _____ and _____, and you don't have a recipe for disaster, but an opportunity for _____ and _____.

9. Champions don't look at what they are going through, but _____ _____.

10. In what ways will hidden sins be found out?
_____
_____
_____

11. Paul encouraged us to wherever possible be on _____ with others.

12. All seeds sown, whether for good or for bad, will _____.

13. What must you permit as a developing leader for yourself and your employees?
_____
_____

14. An employee will only ever know _____, but an employer will know _____.

15. Never settle for knowing _____, always seek the knowing _____.

16. What was Jesus' teaching style?

17. Rather than being vague, how should you handle assignments with your team?

18. How did Christ deal with unethical behaviors in the temple?

19. What guidelines should you follow when dealing with unethical practices in the business arena?

Section 3
Principles of Longevity

20. What has lead to the erosion of morality in our community?
    _____
    _____

21. In your opinion, how has it affected our communities and churches?
    _____
    _____
    _____
    _____

22. What should you build your career around? Why?
    _____
    _____
    _____
    _____

23. You always pay the _____ price for the _____ form of living.

24. In what ways did the love of mammon affect the pharisees?
    _____
    _____
    _____
    _____
    _____

25. What does a "love of money" entail?
   _____
   _____

26. You should see money as a _____ and God as your _____.

27. _____ is something we have, _____ is someone we are.

Section 3
Principles of Longevity

Key Point Review

1. The true gauge of a person's character is given when they give their _____.

2. Having integrity means being true to _____.

3. What happens when you compromise?
    _____
    _____

4. What seems like a recipe for disaster, but will actually be an opportunity for success?
    _____
    _____
    _____

5. What happens with all seeds sown?
    _____
    _____
    _____

6. Explain the importance of teaching others and what it has to do with you as a key leader?
    _____
    _____
    _____
    _____

7. Why should you take the time to teach and train your team?

8. How should you deal with unethical behavior?

9. Why is your destiny not just something you do?

10. What is the difference between your character and your reputation?

11. How can your attitude towards money affect you?

12. What is the difference between wealth and riches?

_____

_____

**Section 3
Principles of Longevity**

Resources of Interest

Character is King
Dr. John Binkley

It's a Guy Thing: Character is King takes you on your dream journey. There is a place called destiny that we all journey to. We all have ideas, dreams and vision for what life should be. This book lays out a plan for that journey to realizing your dreams, to your destiny.

Let's Talk About Sex
Dr. John A. King

Let's face it. Sexuality is all around us. It's even on billboards, and television commercials. Sadly, It's a topic many men have to discover on their own because too many churches or pastors won't touch it. *Let's Talk About Sex* was written so men no longer have to discover the answers to the tough questions about sex on their own.

Now to Next
Dr. John A. King

What does the next generation church look like? Who are the people that will be involved in the next generation church? How will it come about?

Those are some of the questions answered in Dr. King's newest release, *Now to Next: Blueprint for a Christian Revolution*.

Helping Guys Become Men, Husbands, and Fathers
Dr. John A. King

It's a Guy Thing takes you on the journey of fatherhood. Dr. King shows you, in this book, the skills necessary to become a good father. He shows you what can happen when a father is absent or simply not active in a child's life.
Being a male is a matter of birth. Being a man is a matter of choice. This book will help you make that choice.

To see all the titles available through Guy Thing Press, visit us online at www.guythingpress.com

Resources of Interest

Business By The Book
Dr. John A. King

The world's greatest handbook on leadership, economic and social excellence is not found in schoolbooks, but is Scripture. The principles in this book are tried, proven and resilient over centuries. Christ bet His life on it, and so can you.

Show Me the Money
Dr. John A. King

Time Magazine asked, "Does God want you to be rich?" The answer to that question is simply "No, God wants you to be *wealthy*." In *Show Me the Money*, you will learn the fundamentals of creating and using wealth in God's kingdom.

Achieving Authentic Wealth
Jeff McLoud

We need a vision that goes beyond our ability to be consumers only. A vision so big, so powerful, that we cannot even accomplish it in our own lifetime - a vision founded from the very heartbeat of God. We could see the vision fulfilled if we ask ourselves a simple question: "How can we achieve twice as much with half the money?"

Creating a Better Life
Erik A. Kudlis

In this easy to read manual, educator and administrator turned national and international businessman, Erik Kudlis, identifies three vital keys you must know and use, given by God Himself, that unlock the doors to the life God always wanted you to have.

To see all the titles available through Guy Thing Press, visit us online at www.guythingpress.com

Further Resources

The Godly Man Curriculum

The Godly Man Curriculum is the latest development of the International Men's Network. This training curriculum is designed to train men from all walks of life and give them a firm foundation of doctrine and Godly knowledge. This curriculum is available both over the internet for individual study or by DVD for seminars, Sunday schools, and men's meetings. With up to 7 hours of video teaching divided over numerous topics, the Godly Man Curriculum is an excellent tool that you can build your classes upon and grow yourself and your people.

Building Iron Men & Life As Leaders Networks

The Building Iron Men and Life as Leaders networks are two of IMN's finest resources. Each network provides you with a new teaching every month that will challenge and encourage you to grow. The Building Iron Men network features three teachings in both CD and DVD format that focus on your men, while the Life as Leaders network provides you with three CDs that teach you leadership principles you can use in every area of your life.

Both networks are phenomenal tools that are vital assets to any church and discipleship program.

For more information about these and other resources, visit us online at www.imnonline.org

Also check out these websites for great resources and training materials.

International Men's Network
www.imnonline.org

Guy Thing Press
www.guythingpress.com

The International Men's Network was founded by Dr. John A. King. Our purpose as an organization is to help men not only grow to become the leaders their families and churches need, but also become men of God that make a lasting impact on those around them.

IMN is a missionary organization to the men of the world. We are committed to:

- Inspire all men to rise to a high standard of biblical manhood.
- Encourage them to excel in their roles as men, leaders, husbands, and fathers.
- Challenge them to be contributors to society and set an example based upon a biblical value system that will benefit this generation and lay a solid foundation for the next.

As an organization, the International Men's Network is dedicated to providing and hosting the best resources for men, whether it comes from teachings and lessons on CD/DVD format or via a conference that will teach men principles that will help them become more influential and effective in their lives.

For more information about IMN and its mission, visit us online at www.imnonline.org or contact us via phone at 817.993.0047

The Christian Life Center was founded by Dr. John King and his wife, Beccy. With a vision to preach the gospel of Jesus Christ with unashamed passion and uncompromising truth, Christian Life Center aims to raise up the next generation of leaders to move into all the world and proclaim the truth of Christ to the lost and broken.

Located in the Keller, TX area, the Church sits in the prime location to reach the community and the people therein. The Church desires to give back to the community by providing outreaches to better and enrich its inhabitants. From kickboxing classes that are aimed at teaching children and adults self-defense to special service that commemorate and honor our country's war-time heroes, the church strives to bring a living Jesus to a dying world by new and imaginative means that will bless and change lives.

For more information about Christian Life Center and the resources it offers,
visit the website at www.clctx.org

www.ingramcontent.com/pod-product-compliance
Lightning Source LLC
LaVergne TN
LVHW081546060526
838200LV00048B/2230